For all the courageous, brilliant, and kind kids who inspired the following pages.

Special thanks to my three courageous and kind daughters, Molly, Maggie and Madelyn who inspire me every day.
I love you.

Megan Murphy
The Kindness Rocks Project

I

ABOUT

What started as the simple hobby of one quickly spread into an International Kindness movement of many. The Kindness Rocks Project began in 2015 when I began writing inspirational messages for others on beach stones and randomly leaving them around for others to find. I found that my daily hobby of spreading kindness made me happy and it became a personal form of art therapy. I also believe that "One message at just the right moment can change someone's entire day, outlook or life."

As my hobby began to grow, I began planting inspiration gardens flanked by hand-painted driftwood signs describing the idea behind my garden, and I added a call to action for others to join me. As a result, many families followed my lead after returning home from their vacations.

It was then that I realized that I had started a movement. Today, The Kindness Rocks Project can be found in over ninety countries around the world. Families, Schools, Hospitals, Scouting groups, Organizations, and even Fortune 500 Companies around the world are now painting it forward.

As the project began to expand, teachers also reached out to me asking her how they could incorporate the project into their classrooms. I wanted to provide these teachers with tools and supporting social-emotional learning materials to inspire their students. I hired an educational consultant, two videographers, the best IT guy with the biggest heart and a team of creative volunteers willing to help me achieve this goal. Today, teachers around the United States are incorporating The Kindness Rocks Project into their classrooms and using it as an outreach opportunity to spread kindness throughout their communities.

"Tell me and I forget, teach me and I remember, involve me and I learn."
-Benjamin Franklin

Recent studies have shown that social-emotional learning is critical to a child's development and can prepare children to become active members of society and when incorporated in the classroom it can transform schools and the ripple can be felt throughout entire communities.
This book began as a call to action on social media. I asked teachers and parents who are members of The Kindness Rocks Project if they would be willing to participate in a "Kindversations" dialog with their students. One simple Facebook post generated over 200 inquiries. Within these pages, you find the wisdom from their students.
Words we should all live by.

CONTENTS

"Kindness means working hard to make the world a better place."

KATY AGE 12

what does Kindness mean to you? share an example.

1 What Kindness Means To Me

Kindness is the act of caring for others more than you care for yourself. It's putting others first, it's treating others gently and with humility. Kindness takes this bleak world and restores it with hope again." Sara Age 16

To me kindness means being kind helping others, and doing good deeds. Makayla Age 9

Kindness means when I shoveled snow with my friend so a person could get their wheelchair out of the car. Olivia Age 9

Kindness means being nice and standing up for a friend and helping them when they need help. Jayla Age 9

Kindness means being loved, being cared about, and feeling like you have someone to talk to. Takaylah Age 11

Kindness means when my friends help me when I need it. Jack Age 10

Kindness means to me that you are helpful and sweet. Presley Age 9

Kindness means making others feel good and smile!
When someone finds my rock, I will feel happy.
Bailee age 6

Kindness means to me that I am friendly, nice, helpful and many more things. Most of all it makes me feel good. When I do acts of kindness or someone does an act of kindness to me, we both feel good about ourselves. That's what kindness means to me.
By Nadia

To be very nice like hold a door for someone.
Ava Age 10

Being friendly, nice and inclusive.
Jon Age 9

Kindness means you are caring and you want to help someone. If someone thinks you care, they will be touched. Maybe you will create a friendship. That's my way of kindness.
By Luke

If you show someone else kindness they will show it back to you. Jonathan Age 11

It means happiness. Pretend you are walking and an elder person can't cross the roads. You help them and everybody is happy. Daniel Age 11

Giving someone food when they do not have any. Shane Age 8

It is a good feeling! Jake Age 16

Kindness has helped me since I was born. kindness helped me develop a relationship with my family, kindness helped me make friends in Pre - school, and kindness has helped me wherever I go. After all, you can't find perfection anywhere, but kindness is all around the world.- Julie Age 9

4

"KINDNESS TO ME MEANS THAT I HAVE THE CHANCE TO SHOW COMPASSION TO OTHERS, EVEN IF THEY'RE HAVING A BAD DAY OR SOMETHING HAPPENED. IT ALSO MEANS THAT I CAN ACT OUT OF KINDNESS, AND MAYBE THAT WILL AFFECT PEOPLE TO CONTINUE SPREADING KINDNESS, LIKE SPREADING CREAM CHEESE ON A BAGEL THAT IS WHAT KINDNESS MEANS TO ME."

Ethan Age 12

Kindness means to me when people do things to make others feel happy
-Hannah Age 6

BE THE "I" IN KIND
K[I]ND
Name: Lukas   Age: 6

Kindness means standing up for others and if people are lonely play with them.
-Reagan Age 8

Kindness means sharing with others. One time, I shared with my brothers and with my friends. When my friends smiled, it made me happy. I felt so so happy. -Jonah

To me kindness means, making someone happy! If you are kind to one person, it creates a boomerang effect. Meaning, if you are kind to someone, then they might be kind to someone else, and it will keep on going, until eventually, it comes back to you! Same thing with a smile. It can completely change someone's day if you just smile at them. So that is why kindness is so important! It can change a life! -Pablo Age 11

"Think about how someone else would feel in a situation, help someone out of a different situation. When people are having a hard time try to give them advice."

Jonathan Age 11

Ways to show kindness & make other people happy

I tell jokes to friends to cheer them up.
Ava age 8

Be respectful, humble and compromise.
Andrew age 9

When I try to make others happy I give them love and affection, or tell them funny jokers so they can burst with laughter.
Fritz-Nichjolas age 10,

To make others happy I would say beauty comes from the inside out.
Sarah Age 9

Sing Songs
-Nola Age 6

To make others happy I make silly faces, say positive words, and tell so many jokes . I make so many friends because I'm very positive. - AVA Age 10

I put my hand on their back to check on them

Colton Age 6

I make others happy by giving someone a hug and play with them. I let them play with my toys for a day or two or three because that is kind.
Lauren age 6

I help them up if they fall.
Dylan age 6

To make others happy by smiling at them.
Violet age 9

To make others happy, if someone else wants to play something, I would play with them so they do not feel left out.
Chloe age 8

If I had one wish, I would make the world a better place. I would give everyone what they need. I would make sure everyone had a place to call home. Home sweet home.

ALICIA AGE 10

3

If you had one wish what would it be and why?

if you had one wish what would it be?

My one wish would be to see my mom's dad.
Vinny age 9

I would wish for world peace.
Tom age 8

If I had one wish it would be to help out my sister.
Kami age 9

I wish cancer would be eradicated from around the world.
Daniel Age 11

I wish that my house would be made of chocolate coins.
Tony Age 6

My wish is to be a police officer and everyone to be kind and nice to each other and eat hot chicken wings everyday.
Jayla age 8

If I had ONE wish it would be for everyone to live a good and healthy life and to never struggle.
Jacob Age 6

Sometimes we need a little hand.

My wish is for everyone to be accepted.
Mira, Age 12

Equality and world peace and for no one to feel limited by who they are.
Katy Age 12

If I had one wish it would be that all the hatred in the world would cease to exist.
Qwan-Lee Age 9

For everybody to be free from bullying, pain and illness.
Jonathan Age 11

If I had one wish it would be to have the power to change probability. If I had that power, I could have anything from $100 to ending world hunger, just by changing the probability to 100%
Skylar Age 12

My one wish is for my family and friends to be healthy and safe.
Andrew Age 9

"I was brave when my parents split up. I was strong and when I felt down, they encouraged me. We didn't always agree, but they were always right by my side."

Alycea Age 12

Describe a time when you were BRAVE

4

"I came from another country, and I had to adapt to a lot of new things, like a new language, new food, and school."
- Thomas Age 12

I was brave when I had my cochlear implant surgery.
By Ayla Age 9

I was brave when I got my flu shot last year. - Nora Age 9

I was brave when I fought my anxiety disorders to go to school every day and when I stepped on stage and danced my first solo.
Maryella age 10

When I saved a kid from drowning. One day I was swimming and I saw a kid drown. Then I went over there, nobody else saw. Then I went and saved him.
Plenny, age 10

I was brave when I stood up for my sister.
Serenity, age 9

I was brave when the power went off.
Ava age 8

My cousin and I were walking in my backyard and a cat and dog jumped out. They almost hit him, but I went in front of him and I got hit instead of him. I went in front of him on purpose so he wouldn't get hit. Kalin, age 10

I was brave when there was a bear. One day I was fishing with my family. Then I heard a roar and we all got scared. Then we tumbled through the river. Suddenly we jumped out of the water into the trees farther up the mountains. I was scared, but brave.
Emma, 9

When my Meme was sick with cancer and went to heaven.
Phoebe- 7

I AM BRAVE
When I try
new things.
-Katy, age 12

I was brave when my mom had cancer and when I had to get fake teeth.
- Julianne age 9

Describe a time that you were Brave

When someone is kind to me I feel like I am glowing with happiness. I am the sun. I have a great big smile on my face and feel like everything is going my way. Everything will be alright. Happiness is running through my veins. Happiness feels amazing and joyful. I am a glowing hot sun.

Jona age 10

How do you feel when someone is kind to you?

I feel super happy and will be kind back.
Avery age 9

I feel like I'm on top of the world!
Elenor age 9

I feel warm in my heart
Deepti age 11

When someone is kind to me I feel like I matter in this huge world of 7.8 billion people
Qwan-Lee age 9

When someone is kind to me I feel warm and fuzzy inside!
Abigail age 11

When someone is kind to me I feel like I belong. Sarah age 9

When someone is kind to me I feel not alone. Jack age 10

When someone is kind to me it makes me happy, because it makes my day better knowing someone cares about me.
Andrew Age 9

Like I'm being wrapped in a warm hug.
Katy Age 12

I feel so hopeful like anything is possible.
Jonathan Age 11

When Someone Is

I feel good about myself and I feel happy and so many emotions that are related to happy.
Jonathan Age 11

I feel grateful.
Bailey Age 7

Kind To Me

I feel like I'm dancing on a rainbow when someone is kind to me.
Adrian Age 8

I feel like I'm in a soft rainbow.
Mia Age 8

I AM THANKFUL

FOR

MY FAMILY

Ryan Age 10

I am thankful for a roof over my head and family.
Douglas Age 10

My mom because if she didn't have me then I wouldn't be alive.
Emmalyn Age 9

My teachers because they make me learn!
Gabie, Age 6

I am thankful for life.
Jonathan Age 11

I am thankful for my family, my teacher, my dog, my friends and food and water, of course.
Jamison age 10

When I am hungry that I get to eat right away.
Talia age 7

I am thankful because I look smart in my new clothes.
Jake age 16

Good, kind people.
Samantha, age 13

I am thankful for....

I'm thankful for challenges because I can learn from them.
Mira age 12

I am thankful for my education. This makes me thankful because without education I will never go on in life and be brainless forever. Without education I would never have learned what 1 + 1 was and how much money a dollar was. I am thankful for my education.
Toby age 10

I am thankful for people who have high status who are doing good things in the world.
Caroline age 14

THANK YOU!

"If I had a secret super power, it would be for the power to ensure everyone feels supported and loved!"

Maxim Age 12

If you could have one superpower what would it be?

My super power would be to read minds, so I can know what my mom is thinking.
Kyle Age 9

Telekinesis, to fly, and to teleport from place to place -
Luka Age 9

If I could have any secret super power it would be to create secrets to save the world.
Vinny Age 9

If I could have any secret super power it would be super strength, because I can help carry heavy things if people need help.
Jack Age 10

If I could have any secret super power it would be mind reading, because I want to know if people are sad.
Kenyon Age 9

Super Speed so I can run fast to save people in a fire.
Brooklyn Age 6

To make it rain puppies and kittens so everyone could have a pet to love.
Evie Age 6

If you could have any secret super power, what would you want it to be and why?

To stop time so I could stop bad things.
Graden Age 10

To make all my school friends have a good day every day so they are happy:)
Shaunna Age 17

I want to control matter, dark matter anti-matter, cosmic and sonic matter so I can create anything.
Daniel - Age 11

If I could have one super power I would want to have super fast speed because if my parents want me to wake up in the morning for school I can do it at the last minute and rush.
Annaleah, Age 7

Super Powers

To take away people's pain.
-Camilly, age 14

I would want water powers because if an animal got stuck on the beach I could use my water power to cool them off and push them back in the sea.
Aryana age 5

To cure cancer and diseases so people can live longer.
Colin age 10

I would want to be able to fly so I could watch the most beautiful sunsets and be surrounded by clouds.
Kerrin age 10

To be super fast so my brother couldn't catch me.
Alexander age 6

Super hearing, so I could hear whispers about people so I can stand up for them.
Sophia age 8

"I would stop pollution so we can have a happier place to live."

Jenna age 9

If you were in charge of the whole world-what would you do to make the world a happier place?

To make the whole world come together as one and be friends
Maddie age 9

If I was in charge of the world everyone has to be kind and don't call people names.
Olivia age 9

If you were in charge of the whole world, what would you do to make the world a Happier Place?

I would make sure everyone is treated fairly.
Andrew 9

I would make sure there are no homeless people. -
Nora age 9

I would make it so people have equal amounts of money.
Rylan age 10

I would make inventions to make stuff easier.
Jack age 10

I would make a month where everyone has to be nice.
Gage age 10

35

I would pick up trash.
Travis age 9

I would make the world a happier place by trying to stop bullying.
Layna age 9

Get rid of vaping.
Gigi age 9

If I was in charge of the world I would give everybody the biggest slice of a burger and a home for everyone that is homeless.
Nick age 10

"I would make more education and less poverty.
Mason age 9

I would make racism go away to make the world a happier place.
Paul age 10

Give rocks to everyone.
Michael, age 6

I would cancel Monday mornings.
Lena age 7

If I were in charge of the I would make the world happier by telling people to not litter because it is bad for the world. I would also tell them not to hack into computers or phones. Another thing I would do is help people if they lost their favorite necklace, their ring, a phone or their pet.- Isabella age 9

If I could change the world I would make sad things not happen and bring back extinct animals.
Bryce age 9

I would make food free for people who don't have any money.
Sarah age 9

I would get rid of money even though most people say it wouldn't work. I think it would work if we all work together.
Sunny age 10

I would give everyone a hug to cheer them up.
Dara age 7

ART THERAPY
ROCK PAINTING KIT FOR ONE

6+ THE ART OF CONNECTING
ONE FOR ONE, BUY ONE AND WE GIVE ONE TO A PERSON IN NEED

Visit TheKindnessRocksProject.com

Be the "I" in KIND

K ND

Name   Age

SCHOOL(SEL) SOCIAL EMOTIONAL LEARNING PACKAGE

Social & Emotional Learning (SEL) is critical to a child's
development and can prepare children to become active
members of society

and when incorporated in the classroom it can transform
schools!

This educational package was created in collaboration with
an educational curriculum specialist and was tested,

incorporated and proven effective in K-5 Classrooms
around the United States.

For more inspiration or
to participate in our next book
Volume 2

We have Free downloads
for kids & teachers

as well as a social emotional
school presentation package

and additional books &
resources for all ages!

Made in the USA
Middletown, DE
15 April 2021